Pathfinders of the American Frontier

EXPLORATION
AND DISCOVERY

The Conquest of Mexico
The Early French Explorers of North America
Exploration of the California Coast
The Exploration of the Moon
The English Colonization of America
The European Rediscovery of America
Explorers of the American West
Explorers of the South Pacific
The First Voyage Around the World
The Journey of Lewis and Clark
Pathfinders of the American Frontier
The Sea Route to Asia
The Spanish Exploration of Florida
The Spanish Exploration of South America
The Spanish Exploration of the Southwest

EXPLORATION AND DISCOVERY

Pathfinders of the American Frontier

The men who opened the frontier of
North America, from Daniel Boone and
Alexander Mackenzie to Lewis and Clark
and Zebulon Pike

Diane Cook

Mason Crest Publishers
Philadelphia

Mason Crest Publishers
370 Reed Road
Broomall PA 19008

Mason Crest Publishers' world wide web address is
www.masoncrest.com

First printing

1 3 5 7 9 8 6 4 2

Library of Congress Cataloging-in-Publication Data
on file at the Library of Congress

ISBN 1-59084-045-3

EXPLORATION AND DISCOVERY

Contents

Colonists in the Kentucky settlement of Boonesborough (sometimes called Boonesboro) repel attacks by Shawnee Indians during the fall of 1778. The bold frontiersman Daniel Boone had established the settlement three years earlier.

The Siege of Boonesborough

THE MUFFLED SILENCE of snowfall surrounded Daniel Boone as he cut up the buffalo he had just killed. This 400 pounds of meat would go a long way in feeding the 26 men awaiting him at their camp 10 miles away.

Winter was not a good time for so many men to be away from Boonesborough, the settlement that Daniel Boone had established in Kentucky three years earlier, in 1775. But the people at the *garrison* were in dire straits. The Indian "mischiefs," as Boone called them, had made it almost impossible for the settlers to survive the winter. During the summer months of 1777, Native Americans had burned the settlers' corn crops, slaughtered livestock, and left the newcomers almost nothing to eat. Times were hard with no bread, vegetables, fruit, or alcohol. The settlers only had meat, and sometimes even that was scarce. Furthermore, salt was necessary to preserve the meat, and they had little. In the Kentucky of 1778, a bushel of this **preservative** was worth more than a cow.

So Boone led 30 men from Boonesborough on January 6 to gather salt at the Lower Blue Licks of the Licking River. The men would boil the salty water, which would evaporate, leaving salt behind. They needed to boil about 84 gallons of water to get a bushel of salt at Lower Blue Licks, and the spring discharged about 10,000 gallons of **brine** daily. The men worked at an exhausting pace, producing about 10 bushels of salt a day. Some collected brine while others chopped wood, hauled fuel, tended fires, or scraped salt residue from the sides of the kettles.

After gathering several hundred bushels, Boone sent half of the men back to the garrison with the salt. The rest intended to continue working. However, the river was rising. When the floodwaters submerged the spring, their work had to stop. Because all they could do was wait, Boone, his son-in-law Flanders Callaway, and Thomas Brooks took hunting trips to find food for the camp.

The hunters had to be careful, because the American Revolution was in full swing. While they saw few Redcoats

Daniel Boone

Daniel Boone was born in Berks County, Pennsylvania in 1734 to Squire and Sarah Morgan Boone. He was one of 11 children.

Daniel grew up preferring hunting rather than farming. At 15, he was one of the area's best woodsmen. He was so comfortable on the trails that he guided his family's move to North Carolina in 1750.

When Daniel, 21, courted 17-year-old Rebecca Bryan in the summer of 1756, he measured five feet eight inches tall and weighed 175 pounds. He was powerfully built with broad shoulders, penetrating blue-gray eyes, a fair and ruddy complexion, a tight wide mouth, and a long slender nose. His dark hair was braided in Indian fashion. Daniel and Rebecca were married on August 14 and later had 10 children—six boys and four girls.

In 1784, journalist John Filson published a book immortalizing Daniel as "the first American backwoods literary hero." Daniel moved his family to Kentucky in 1778 and then to Missouri in 1799 where he remained until Rebecca died in March 1813. Boone continued exploring the west after this, until he died in 1820. He was 85.

beyond the Cumberland Gap, the British did pay Indians to harass and kill settlers. One of the most hated British leaders was in Detroit—Governor Henry Hamilton, better

The year before Boone and his men went to Blue Lick to gather salt, the Shawnee attacks on white settlers had been fierce. The Kentucky settlers called 1777 the "year of the bloody sevens."

known as the Hair Buyer since he paid for settlers' scalps as proof of their demise.

The Indians didn't need reasons like this to go after the settlers, however. Colonists earned the Shawnee tribe's wrath because of the unprovoked murder of the Shawnee chief Cornstalk and three other natives who had not taken sides during the war.

On this snowy day, the fighting was on the other side of the Cumberland Gap. Daniel felt secure in the snow since it was common knowledge that large groups of Indians did not move around in the winter. About an inch of snow had fallen by the time Daniel tied the last of the buffalo meat on his horse. Then, he saw four Indian braves watching him. Escape was futile since he could be easily tracked in the fresh snow, but he tried.

"By this time, the Indians were very close," Daniel's son, Nathan Boone, told Lyman Copeland Draper about 64 years later. "He could not get his horse unloaded to escape. Thus, his only chance was to dart off on foot. After running about a half a mile or thereabouts, the Indians approached close and commenced firing at him. Father believed they did not intend to kill him, as several balls struck on either side of him close by, knocking up the snow. They then came within eight or ten paces and fired another volley. One ball cut the strap of his powder horn loose. He believed they might easily have killed him.

"Eventually, he was too tired to run farther, and as the Indians were gaining on him, he decided that it would be impossible to escape. He then dodged behind a tree and placed his gun by the side of the tree, leaning against it, in plain view, as a token of surrender. The Indians came up, whooping and laughing, in view of their success, and took his gun, knife, and ammunition."

The small hunting party took Daniel to their main camp, where he was surprised to find more than 100 Shawnee and Delaware warriors and some French woodsmen. He recognized Captain Will, a Delaware chief who had released Daniel from captivity on two other occasions. Blackfish was the main chief. Pompey, an African American who had been captured by the Shawnee when he was a child, translated for Blackfish and Daniel.

> When Daniel Boone spoke to Captain Will, the chief did not recognize him at first. After Boone reminded Captain Will that he had captured Boone eight years earlier on the Kentucky River, the chief recalled the incident.

Why did Daniel Boone agree to surrender his men at the Lower Blue Licks? His son later explained, "I think my father's reason for surrendering his men was knowing that with several inches of snow upon the ground, if they attacked, none would be able to escape, [as the Indians could follow their trails in the snow]. The enemy had four times as many men as the salt boilers, and the latter, ignorant of their presence, would find it impossible to escape. He also knew the next day would be Sunday, so when the Indians arrived, his men would be loitering about and off their guard."

Using Pompey as an interpreter, Blackfish asked if the men at the Lower Blue Licks were with Daniel. When Daniel said yes, Blackfish said the Indians were going to kill them. Daniel then made a deal with the Indians. He promised that the men would surrender without a fight if the Indians would neither mistreat them nor make them run the *gauntlet*. The Indians agreed.

Twenty-six men were taken prisoner the next day. When the Indians arrived, the snow was half-a-leg deep. Daniel called out to his men and told them they were surrounded, that it would be impossible to get away, explained the *stipulation* for surrender, and begged them to make no attempt to defend themselves.

The Indians took their prisoners, some kettles, and axes and started the long march to their camp. That night, the Indians began to clear the snow and make a path about 100 yards long. Daniel asked Pompey what they were doing. He told Daniel the cleared area was for running the gauntlet.

"My father reminded Blackfish of his promise not to make the prisoners run the gauntlet," Nathan Boone said. "Blackfish told him it was not for his men, who had capitulated, but for himself, who had been captured and had made no such stipulation.

"Blackfish said he could run the gauntlet there immediately or wait till he reached the Indian towns. Father chose to run the gauntlet immediately. The line was formed. Some of the Indians had clubs or sticks, and some had tomahawks. And Father ran. The Indians made great motions as if they would split his brains out, but seemed to favor him; he only received a few slight strokes from switches."

After a 10-day march to Old Chillicothe on the Little Miami River, the Shawnee formally adopted 16 of the men into the tribe. Boone became the son of Blackfish. In March 1778, the rest of the captives were released to

Governor Hamilton in Detroit, where the British paid $100 for each American prisoner. Daniel and the other 15 men who had been adopted remained with the tribe.

Daniel pretended to be satisfied with his new life with the tribe, and he gained more and more freedom. After the trek to Detroit, Daniel learned the Delaware chiefs were planning to attack Boonesborough. In mid-June, he slipped away while Blackfish and his braves were hunting.

Daniel road his pony until it collapsed the next morning. Then he ran until his feet were raw. When he came to the Ohio River, Daniel built a makeshift raft to carry his clothes, rifle, and ammunition. He then swam to the other side behind the raft. From there, he continued to the garrison. On June 20, breathless, exhausted, and famished, Daniel reached Boonesborough. Imagine his disappointment when he learned that his wife, Rebecca, had taken the family back to her father's house in North Carolina. Only his daughter, Jemima, remained in the garrison with her husband, Flanders Callaway, who had been hunting when the other salt boilers were captured.

Boone immediately put people to work preparing for the attack. On September 7, 1778, about 400 Indians and 40 Frenchmen showed up at Boonesborough. After about four days of negotiation, the two sides reached a tentative peace agreement. But then violence erupted.

This drawing from a 19th-century book shows Daniel Boone's settlement at Boonesborough. The buildings were constructed so they could be used to defend against attacks by hostile Native Americans.

"This council was to be closed with handshaking, with two Indians to each white man," Nathan Boone said. "Then one Indian locked his right arm with a white man's left hand and shook the white man's left; and the other Indian in the same manner on the white man's right. Blackfish was one of those who shook hands with my father. But treachery took place, and a scuffle ensued. Father threw Blackfish flat on the ground, and the other Indian let go his hold. At this instant, the other Indian, who seems to have carried the pipe tomahawk around for smoking in the council, now aimed a blow at Father. He partly dodged the blow, but the handle struck the back of his head, cutting through the skin. The wound was over two inches long and left a scar over which hair didn't grow. It appeared from the scar that he was leaning in a bending posture in front, as the blade cut a lesser wound between the shoulders, but he escaped."

There was fierce fighting on both sides. The *siege* lasted 11 days. The Indians fired rifles at the Boonesborough defenders. They shot flaming arrows, hoping the homes would catch on fire. They also tried to tunnel under the stockade walls. Blackfish was fatally wounded during the siege and died several weeks later. Inside, two men died defending the fort, including an African American named

Daniel Boone's daughter Jemima was wounded during the siege of Boonesborough. She was shot in the back. Fortunately, the musket ball had lost most of its force by the time it hit her. "When Jemima received the spent ball in her back, she was dressed only in her underclothes and petticoat," one eyewitness later reported. "The ball drove the cloth into the fleshy part of her back, but the cloth was not broken, so the ball was easily pulled out by pulling the cloth out."

David Bundrin. "David Bundrin was shot in the forehead and died the third day," Nathan Boone said later. "The Negro had dug a hole under the sill of his house and was crawling partially out to get good shots at Indians during the night. But they located him by flashes of his gun and crept up and tomahawked him."

The Shawnee launched their final assault on September 17, 1778. The Indians rushed the fort with large torches and started numerous fires, but a heavy rain later that evening extinguished them. There was so much shooting on both sides that the exploding powder brilliantly lit the night sky. The settlers killed more Indians during this assault than in all the previous days of the siege. The next morning, the settlers discovered the Shawnee camp empty. The Indians were pulling out.

The Shawnee lost about 37 men. Around the fort's walls, settlers found enough spent balls to equal 125 pounds of lead. Boonesborough had withstood the test of Indian attack.

With the fort secure, Daniel went to North Carolina to retrieve the rest of his family. They returned to Boonesborough in the fall of 1779.

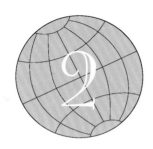

The Wilderness Road

AMERICA. THIS NEW frontier's call drew Europeans in droves during the mid-18th century. In 1700, about 250,000 settlers called the original 13 colonies home. By 1750, the population had more than quadrupled and it would double again over the next 20 years. By 1800, five million people lived in the United States.

The wilderness represented a new type of freedom to the land-starved Europeans who came to America. It seemed to be a land of milk and honey. Sailors even said they could smell the fragrance of pine trees 180 nautical miles offshore as their ships neared port. Stories circulated of the country having so many trees that a squirrel could scamper from the

Atlantic Ocean to the Great Lakes without ever touching the ground.

Before 1750, settlers seemed to be content with remaining in the 13 original colonies. Their presence, however, had a disastrous effect on the regions' original inhabitants. Imported diseases, such as **smallpox**, wiped out almost 90 percent of the natives in the Susquehanna and Delaware River region. Yet in Pennsylvania, the Indians and colonists traded goods and services on a regular basis.

Traders were doing business with Indians in the area now known as Kentucky well before 1734. **Commerce** became the order of the day as merchants bought animal skins from both the Indians and the settlers. Deerskin was an important part of the colonists' economy. In 1753, more than 30,000 deerskins were exported from North Carolina. The colony used thousands more for leggings, **breeches**, and moccasins. By 1750, the skin of a buck, or male deer, served as a unit of trade. One "buck" was equal to a Spanish peso, which was also called by its German name, the "thaler," or dollar.

When deer herds around the colonies started dwindling, trappers and traders started pushing westward in search of game and, eventually, land. But the 100,000 Native Americans in their 26 tribes in the western regions did not want to compete with colonists. This often led to brutal

A colored drawing of a fur trapper in the North American wilderness. Trappers spent months in the woods, returning to the "civilized" areas of the east only after they had collected enough furs to be able to sell for a good profit—much of which they spent on supplies for their next trip into the woods.

attacks and raids as each side tried to gain dominance over the other.

Bands of Indian warriors were known to leave their western towns on the Ohio River and travel south along the Great Warrior's Path that ran down the west flank of the Appalachian Mountains. They would cross through the Cumberland Gap to the Atlantic side and attack settlements in the interior valleys. In 1753, a Shawnee war party took this route and hit near the Forks of the Yadkin River.

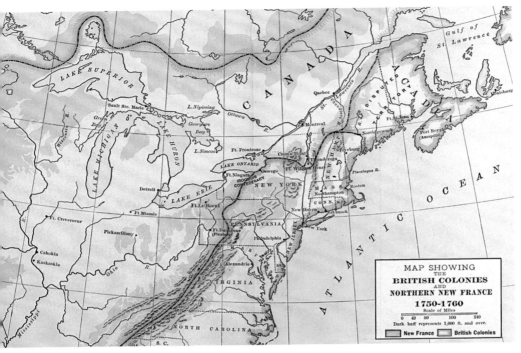

This map of the northeastern area of what today is the United States shows the location of the English colonies in North America. In October 1763, the British government issed a proclamation that prohibited settlements west of the Appalachian Mountains. Despite this order, many white settlers pushed over the mountains or through the Cumberland Gap to establish frontier settlements.

They destroyed many isolated cabins before the Catawba Indians and the county militia drove them away.

The Shawnee Indians claimed the land between the Ohio and the Cumberland rivers, which they called the Shawnee River, as their homeland. Displaced by the Iroquois who attacked the Ohio Valley in the 1680s, the Shawnee then moved into Pennsylvania. The colonists' *encroachment*, however, drove them back to the plains north of the junction of the Red and Kentucky Rivers until 1750. At its peak, one of the Shawnee towns had about 1,000 residents.

In 1767, Daniel Boone visited the Kentucky area twice. On his way back from the first trip, some Cherokees robbed him of all his furs. That fall, Daniel and his brother, Squire, and William Hill set out for a longer journey. They followed the Kentucky River and wintered on the far side of the Blue Ridge Mountains.

Kanta-ke **was the Iroquois term meaning meadows or fields. From it came the name for the region, Kentucky. Colonial soldiers during the French and Indian War learned about the western lands. Around campfires, the men talked about the land with its rich soil for planting, navigable waterways, natural salt licks, and game-filled forests.**

The next winter, a woodsman named John Finley, who had married one of Daniel's sisters, told Daniel he wanted to find the Warriors Path. This was a route that took the Cherokees through a mysterious gap in the Cumberland Mountains into Kentucky. The Cherokee used the pass to attack their northern enemies. It was Finley's dream to find this pass that, he believed, would be crucial in opening up trade in the Ohio country. In May 1769, Daniel, Finley, John Stuart, Joseph Holden, William Cooley, and Ames

Mooney left to find the Cumberland Gap.

> Daniel Boone and his men were not the first white men through the Cumberland Gap. A Virginia land speculator named Dr. Thomas Walker, had stumbled upon the gap in 1750.

Daniel found the trail and led the men through the natural pass between what is now the southwestern tip of Virginia and Middlesborough, Kentucky.

Daniel and his men settled at a place they called Station Creek Camp and started gathering furs to take back home. The group split up to cover more ground, and in December, Daniel and Stuart were captured by a party of Delaware warriors led by a chief known as Captain Will. The Indians took their *pelts*, skins, guns, ammunition, and equipment and warned them not to return to the area. Daniel and Stuart were left with cheap guns normally used to trade with the Native Americans (the colonists did not want to give their best weapons to the Native Americans). They also had a small amount of ammunition, and a pair of spare moccasins. They managed to track the Indians and steal back some horses and pelts before they were recaptured. This time, the Indians took the two men to the Ohio River before releasing them.

When the two men met other members of their party, Daniel was glad to see that Squire had joined them with fresh horses, guns, ammunition, and traps. Daniel decided

This famous painting by George Caleb Bingham shows Daniel Boone leading a group of settlers into Kentucky along the Wilderness Road.

to remain in Kentucky and explore some more. He was away from his family for almost two years.

Daniel returned to Kentucky with five men from North Carolina in the fall of 1772. That winter, they transported their pelts along the river.

Kentucky drew others to its fertile lands as well. In 1772, George Rogers Clark, then 19, left Pittsburgh in a canoe and paddled about 300 miles down the Ohio River where he staked a claim to some land.

People in the seaboard colonies were starting to get excited about Kentucky. James and Robert McAffee from Virginia and James Harrod from Pennsylvania led two separate surveying parties late in 1773.

On September 25, 1773, Daniel led a group of about 50 people who wanted to settle in Kentucky. They were encroaching on territory claimed by both the Cherokee and the Shawnee tribes. Daniel was warned to stay away or suffer the consequences.

Daniel was concerned about having enough provisions for the journey. He sent his oldest son, James, along with John and Richard Mendenhall from North Carolina to arrange for additional supplies at Castle's Wood.

On October 3, 1773, James Boone, the Mendenhall boys, and the rest of the party, which included two other white men and two African Americans, were camped for the night about three miles behind Daniel Boone's camp. Nineteen Indians—15 Delaware, two Cherokee, and two Shawnee—overran the camp. Although some members of the party escaped, James and the Mendenhall boys were brutally tortured and killed as a message to other settlers to stay out of Kentucky. One man watched the scene unfold from a hiding place in the underbrush. The Indians took Charles, one of the black men, with them.

When Daniel found James, John, and Richard, he

James Harrod

Although Daniel Boone may be the most famous frontiersman of colonial America, he was not the first man to explore central Kentucky. In 1767, a 25-year-old Pennsylvanian named James Harrod explored the forests along the Kentucky River. Seven years later, he returned by canoe with 32 men. They cleared land, laid out streets, and established a small settlement, which they called Harrodsburg. This was the first town established in Kentucky.

In 1775, Daniel Boone came to Harrodsburg to warn the settlers about an impending attack by Shawnee Indians. For the next several years, the settlers and Native Americans fought a series of fierce battles, culminating in the "year of the bloody sevens"—1777. At one crucial point, the fort at Harrodsburg was surrounded by hostile Shawnee braves and the settlers were nearly out of gunpowder and musket balls. James Harrod and 30 men snuck past the attackers to retrieve the settlers' hidden supply of gunpowder, saving the fort.

Unlike most woodsmen of the time, Harrod was able to read and write. He would go on to found a school in Kentucky, and to be elected to the Virginia legislature in 1779 and 1784.

In 1791 he left home to search for a silver mine, but was never heard from again. His family believed that Harrod had been murdered by settler who was angry about a land claim.

> **The frontiersman George Rogers Clark would become an American hero of the Revolution. His younger brother, William, gained fame as one of the leaders of the Lewis and Clark Expedition from 1804–06.**

wrapped their bodies in linen sheets and buried them where they had died. Disheartened, the settlers returned to North Carolina. The brutal murders turned many people against the Indians and brought about fierce retaliations against the Indians, regardless of tribal affiliations. This helped start Lord Dunmore's War between the colonists and the Indians, a war characterized by brutality and ferocity on both sides.

Late in 1774, the colonists won a deciding victory against the Indians at the battle of Point Pleasant in what is now West Virginia. The Shawnee agreed to a treaty that would allow for the settlement of the Ohio Valley.

In March 1775, Daniel led settlers under the authority of the Transylvania Company to Boonesborough, a site on the south bank of the Kentucky River. During the trip, the settlers blazed what later became known as the Wilderness Road, a narrow trail over heavy wooded ridges. This became a primary road to the west. By June 14, the road and three sides of the Boonesborough *stockade* were finished.

Disputes arose between several states over who had claim to Kentucky and the Ohio Valley. These disputes were complicated in April 1775 by the outbreak of the American Revolution between Britain and the 13 colonies. The British used the Indians to wage war against the colonists in the westernmost regions. Afraid of these attacks, many of the Kentucky settlers returned to the other side of the Appalachian mountains. Historical reports indicate that by August 1775, not more than 50 men remained in Kentucky.

Despite of the danger, Daniel brought his family to Boonesborough in the autumn of 1775. The families at the garrison had survived Indian attacks and remained despite many hardships.

When George Rogers Clark won a series of victories over British forces under Governor Henry Hamilton on the frontier between 1778 and 1782, the settlers felt the worst was over. In 1779, about 20,000 colonists moved into Kentucky using both the Ohio River and the Wilderness Road as access points. Some started settlements as far west as Nashville, Tennessee. This began a push westward that would not end until the country was settled from coast to coast.

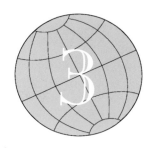

Traversing the Continent

WHILE THE COLONISTS were taming the Atlantic coast, the French were adapting to the Canadian northwest. Canada's harsh climate and quality of soil was not good for farming. However, the Canadian wilderness was filled with muskrat, otter, marten, mink, bear, fox, wolf, lynx, buffalo, and beaver—animals which could be trapped for their valuable furs. The French settlers quickly adapted to this new environment and became adept trappers and traders.

Since 1670, the Hudson Bay Company had a monopoly on the New World's fur trade. At that time, King Charles II of England granted it the rights to an area that included 1.5 million square miles of present-day Canada. The trading company established posts throughout the region where furs and pelts could be collected and sent overseas.

Between 1750 and 1780, Canadian and Scottish traders created alliances and formed the North West Company. This was in direct competition with the Hudson Bay Company. This competition played an important part in the exploration and expansion of Canada.

Like other colonists in the New World, the French developed their own unique ways of treating the natives. In Mexico and South America, the Spanish enslaved the Indians. In North America, the British drove them from their hunting grounds. In Canada, the French married their women and adopted many of the natives' ways. The French trappers soon became masters of the wilderness. They were called *coureurs de bois*, or woods runners, and could travel the area freely and trade with their Indian friends. These Frenchmen could live off the land and use birchbark canoes to cross the region's many rivers and lakes. Many of them remained in the wilderness, even even after the France surrendered Canada to England in 1763.

Fur traders and trappers soon journeyed into the interior in a search for more furs. In 1774, Joseph Frobisher found a route that led to the richest fur fields of all.

As the trappers traveled deeper into Canada, it became more expensive to bring the furs out to the large markets on

The coat of arms for the Hudson's Bay Company, circa 1780. Beginning in the mid-17th century, the fur-trading stations of the Hudson's Bay Company did business throughout the vast northwestern regions of Canada.

the eastern coast. Many people wanted to find a route to the Pacific Ocean. This way, ships could pick up the furs and take them to markets in Russia, Asia, and Europe. This would help the trading companies reduce costs and make their ventures more profitable.

The English wanted to find an overland route to the Pacific for political reasons as well. The king of England was feeling pressure to establish his place in North America. The Spanish were already trying to claim parts of the Pacific coast of North America. The Russians, who lived farther north, might soon be a threat to the coastline as they expanded their territory. The Americans, to the south, were also showing signs of expansion. To ensure its claim to Canada, England needed to develop permanent sites along the western coast of North America.

In 1771, Hudson Bay Company's Samuel Hearne discovered the Coppermine River and followed it to the Arctic Ocean. He concluded that no overland route to the Pacific existed far enough south to be worthwhile. Many disagreed. The British Admiralty even sent Captain James Cook of the Royal Navy to explore the coast in 1778. While Cook did not find the passage, he did find Russians trading great amounts of marine furs—seal and otter—with China.

North West Company officials sent trading parties consisting of a partner, or *bourgeois*, a clerk, an interpreter, a guide, and several dozen canoemen, or *voyageurs*, to purchase furs from Indians and trappers.

Before the colonists arrived, the Native Americans were self-sufficient and provided for themselves everything they

Samuel Hearne made several exploratory trips through Canada for the Hudson's Bay Company during the 1770s. In 1770 he explored the west coast of Hudson's Bay, then traveled inland to Dubawnt Lake. For the next two years he explored the Coppermine River and the Great Slave Lake. In 1774, he established a trading post on the Saskatchewan River.

needed. Soon, however, they began to rely on newly introduced Western products. In addition to alcohol, the traders sold Indians a variety of things, such as cloth, blankets, clothing, guns, ammunition, knives, axes, kettles, tobacco, beads, and paint.

> The *voyageurs,* lower-ranking crewmen often of mixed European and Indian blood, were generally the lowest-paid members of the party. The partners and clerks were normally British or Scottish.

Many names stand out during these years of exploration, but Peter Pond is one that figures prominently in both the fur-trading business and the Northwest expansion. In 1785, he joined the North West Company and was soon sent to Athabasca to organize the district. It soon became one of the region's most important trading posts. Though often occupied with the business of trading, Pond had a strong desire to see what lay beyond his district.

Based on various reports from the natives, Pond pieced together a remarkably accurate map to the West Coast. Unfortunately, it became incorrect when he changed his map after reading reports from the 1778 voyage of Captain James Cook. The error occurred because when Captain Cook discovered a long inlet along the Alaskan coast (which is now named for him), he incorrectly thought a large river must empty there. Because of Cook's mistake,

Pond reported that the Great Slave Lake flowed southwest, when in fact it flowed north. This made Pond's map wrong.

Shortly after Pond arrived at Athabasca, a **rival** firm, the newly formed XY Company, opened shop. John Ross, the rival's representative in Athabasca, was killed in a fight with Pond's men during the winter of 1786–87. The company soon merged with North West Company and sent Alexander Mackenzie, to join Pond as a representative.

Mackenzie arrived October 27, 1787. During his winter at Athabasca, Mackenzie learned all he could about the country and, in the process, caught Pond's passion for exploration. Pond's departure from the Northwest the following year left the area wide open for Mackenzie, whose first exploration took him down the river that flowed out of Slave Lake. Following the river revealed that Pond's theories about Cook's river were wrong.

Mackenzie's cousin, Roderick, took over the duties at the trading post while Alexander prepared for his first expedition to find the Pacific. On June 3, 1789, he set out on his voyage. Four French Canadians, two with their wives; a German; an Indian named English Chief and his two wives; and two of his followers, along with Mackenzie, occupied three canoes loaded for the trip. Three weeks into a rugged and harsh journey, they came upon a lake, now called the Mackenzie. On July 2, they saw a chain of mountains that

Alexander Mackenzie

Alexander, the son of Kenneth Mackenzie and Isabella Maciver, was born in 1764 on Lewis Island in Scotland. After Isabella died, Kenneth moved to New York, where his brother-in-law John was a successful merchant. Both Kenneth and John joined the British army at the outset of the Revolutionary War in 1776. Two years later, Alexander was sent to Montreal, Quebec, for safety.

At age 15, Mackenzie became a clerk for Finlay, Gregory & Company, a small trading company that eventually merged with the North West Company.

In 1787, Mackenzie, now a minor partner, was sent to the Athabasca region, where he met Peter Pond. Pond's influence sparked Mackenzie's desire to find an overland route to the Pacific. His first expedition led him to the Arctic Ocean. After 18 months in England to study advances in navigation, Mackenzie returned to America and successfully crossed the North American continent.

In 1802, he was knighted. Sir Alexander Mackenzie served on the Legislative Assembly of Lower Canada from 1804 to 1808. He married in 1812 and soon moved to Scotland, where he died in 1820.

formed a continuous barrier westward. Called the Mackenzie Mountains, they are now known to be part of the Rocky Mountain chain. The farther north the expedition traveled, the clearer it became that they were not on Cook's river. Along the way, the group encountered primitive Indians who fed them. These Indians were afraid of the Eskimos, who would kill them.

During the 102-day trip, Mackenzie traveled almost 3,000 miles, discovered a major river, reached the Arctic Ocean, and saw country never before seen by Europeans. However, he had to turn back before he reached the Pacific.

Mackenzie was not discouraged. He decided to leave Canada and spend the winter of 1791 studying in London. His decision was made after conferring with a Hudson Bay Company surveyor, who suggested that Mackenzie learn enough astronomy to determine **longitude**. Mackenzie also needed to buy suitable instruments for making observations before continuing his next journey.

After learning these new skills and buying equipment, Mackenzie left England on May 9, 1792, to return to Canada. He landed in Montreal and went from there to Grand Portage and then to Athabasca. He had a telescope, a sextant, a compass, a **chronometer**, the knowledge of two different methods for calculating longitude, and a portable clock that kept accurate time.

On October 10, he left Athabasca. This time, he took the Peace River and headed west, then south, then west again. He spent the winter 260 miles downriver. He had seven *voyageurs* with him: Jacque Beauchamp, Francois Beaulieux, Baptiste Bisson, Francois Courtois, Joseph Landry, Charles Ducette, and Alexander Mackay. This second expedition left its winter quarters on May 9, 1793.

Seventy-four days later, on July 22, 1793, they reached the Pacific Coast. Mackenzie recorded his arrival by painting his name, the date, and an affirmation that he had arrived by land on the boulder. The 1,200-mile return trip took 33 days.

Though Mackenzie's exploration added new territory to the North West Company, some of his partners were angry because he brought back no furs and he promoted the idea of developing a harbor on the west coast to set up trade with China. Mackenzie further recommended the merger of the North West Company and the Hudson Bay Company, with London personnel running the operation. Some of his partners were strongly opposed to the idea. When Mackenzie's partnership agreement expired in 1797, he left the company and returned to London, where he received a hero's welcome.

The Journey of Lewis and Clark

THE BRITISH were not the only people with an eye on Mackenzie and his accomplishments. Thomas Jefferson, who became America's third president in 1801, also watched the mission closely. He was encouraged by Mackenzie's discovery but wanted to start an American-led effort.

When the United States completed the Louisiana Purchase in 1803, it more than doubled in size. The 820,000 square miles of the Louisiana Territory included the modern-day states of Louisiana, Arkansas, Missouri, Iowa, Wisconsin, Minnesota, North Dakota, South Dakota, Nebraska, Kansas, Oklahoma, Colorado, Wyoming, and Montana. Jefferson immediately wanted to send scouts into the western frontier to find out exactly what the United States had bought from France for about $15 million. Jefferson chose his secretary, 29-year-old Meriwether Lewis, to head up the expedition. Jefferson had been grooming Lewis for this project since 1801.

Lewis gathered an assortment of weapons, navigational instruments, and gifts to trade with the Indians for the trip. Jefferson was adamant about establishing friendly relations with the Indians. Lewis also wrote to his former Army commander, 33-year-old William Clark, and asked him to join the expedition. Though Congress would only give Clark the rank of lieutenant while Lewis was a captain, they both agreed to share command of the expedition.

On July 5, 1803, Lewis left Washington, D.C. and headed west to Pittsburgh. There, a 55-foot **keelboat** was built that would carry most of the members of their expedition. The boat could carry 10 tons of provisions and was supplied with oars, sails, and ropes for towing it from the banks. Lewis also purchased two 50-foot *pirogues*—boats made by hollowing large tree trunks—and a big Newfoundland dog named Seaman.

Lewis left Pittsburgh in October and took the Ohio River to pick up Clark and men recruited for the expedition. In all, they had about 40 soldiers and several French guides. Clark's African-American slave, York, was also part

Among the items which Lewis and Clark took with them on their journey west were peace medals, which they were told to give to the Native American leaders they met. Despite the damage to this medal, the motto "peace and friendship" can still be seen. The reverse side showed a picture of President Jefferson.

of the expedition. Together, these men comprised the Corps of Discovery.

Once loaded, the boat headed to St. Louis and the mouth of the Missouri River. It was December 1803. Since they couldn't travel far in the winter, Clark set up a base of operations called Camp Dubois, or Camp Wood, opposite the mouth of the Missouri River. They built a small fort there where Clark started training the men.

On the afternoon of May 14, 1804, the journey finally began. Since they were traveling northwest, they were going against the river's current. This meant they had to propel the boat through the water by rowing. Despite the heat, the insects, and the backbreaking work, they traveled 642 miles by July 21.

The terrain changed sufficiently at this point and offered all sorts of wonders. Descriptions of new and strange

Meriwether Lewis

Meriwether Lewis was born August 18,1774, to William and Lucy Meriwether Lewis on a Virginia plantation. His father, a Continental Army officer, died in 1779.

Meriwether's strong character was revealed at a young age. When he was eight, Lewis was returning home from a hunt. He and his friends were crossing a field when a bull charged the group. Young Lewis calmly pulled his rifle to his shoulder, aimed, and killed the animal. Thomas Jefferson, who would become the third U.S. president, often praised the youngster for his enterprise, boldness, and discretion.

In 1801, while a captain in the United States Army, Lewis became private secretary to President-elect Jefferson, who invited him to lead an expedition to explore a western route to the Pacific Coast. Lewis asked his friend William Clark to share command of the expedition.

In 1807, President Jefferson named Lewis governor of the Louisiana Territory. He died in 1809.

animals, such as prairie dogs, pronghorn antelopes, and jackrabbits, filled the explorers' notebooks. Members of the Corps of Discovery spent a full day pouring buckets of water into a prairie dog's large nest. Once the very wet prairie dog, or barking squirrel as the crew called it, emerged from its tunnels, it joined a collection of birds, animals, and

William Clark

William Clark, born in 1779 in Caroline County, Virginia, was the youngest of six brothers, one of whom was George Rogers Clark, a noted Revolutionary War soldier. His family moved to Kentucky when he was young.

William co-commanded the famous Lewis and Clark Expedition with Meriwether Lewis from 1804 to 1806. Lewis, who had served with Clark in the U.S. Army, invited him to be a part of the expedition. A tough woodsman accustomed to command, Clark was known for his ability to lead enlisted men. He was a good surveyor, mapmaker, and waterman and served as the Corps of Discovery's record keeper.

In 1807, President Thomas Jefferson appointed Clark superintendent of Indian affairs for the Louisiana Territory with the rank of brigadier general of the militia. After Lewis' death in 1809, Clark assumed responsibility for the publication of the expedition's journals. He died in 1838.

plants—both alive and dead—that would be sent back to the president after winter encampment.

By October 25, 1804, the corps reached its winter destination with the peaceful Mandan Indians. They had traveled 1,600 miles in 164 days. The corps built its winter fort across from the Mandan village in what is now North Dakota. They remained at the fort for five months. Here, they met a woman who would become one of the most valued members of the expedition—Sacagawea, the wife of a French-Canadian trader named Toussaint Charbonneau.

Born a Shoshone Indian, Sacagawea had been captured by the Hidatsa Indians when she was 13. In February 1805, her son, Jean Baptiste, was born. Sacagawea carried him all the way to the Pacific and back again. Because she accompanied the men, Indian tribes knew the Corps of Discovery was peaceful, because war parties never included women.

When the corps left its winter quarters, about a fourth of the crew returned to St. Louis in the keelboat to deliver the notes and specimens, including four live magpies and the prairie dog, to President Jefferson. During this first leg of the journey, the corps had traveled to places that other white men had traveled to. The next leg of the journey would take them into the unknown.

Around 4 P.M. on April 7, 1805, the corps' 33 members continued up the Missouri River and westward into the area

Lewis and Clark, in the distance at the right, meet a group of Shoshone Indians while on their way west. The Shoshone gave the explorers horses, and several joined the party as guides to help them through the mountains.

now known as Montana. They encountered more strange animals, such as bighorn sheep and grizzly bears. In early June, they found another river, the Marias, merging with the Missouri. After scouting ahead, they decided to take the left branch, which took them to the Falls of the Missouri. The corps left the two pirogues behind, buried non-essential equipment near the falls, and made wagon frames to carry several Indian-made canoes. It took a month to *circumnavigate* the falls. On the other side, they found a magnificent canyon at the foot of the Rockies. Sacagawea recognized landmarks from her childhood.

While some of the men scouted a branch of the river they named the Jefferson, Lewis went looking for the Shoshone. When they finally met, he convinced them to return with him to camp. Once there, Sacagawea recognized the tribal chief. He was her brother, Cameahwait. The Shoshone sold horses to the corps and elicited promises to purchase guns from the United States so they could fight their enemies—the Sioux and the Blackfeet.

When the corps set out again, they would still have to cross the Bitterroot Range of the Rocky Mountains that separates what is now Montana and Idaho. Instead of a river route, the co-commanders decided to follow a Shoshone guide, Old Toby, across the mountains on horseback. They

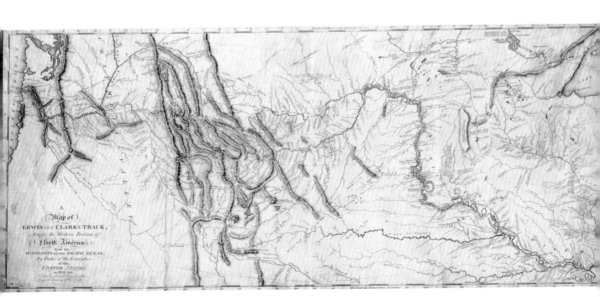

This map of Lewis and Clark's route to the Pacific Ocean was drawn in 1814. It was based on Clark's notes and journals.

soon discovered that he had a tendency to get lost. On August 30, 1805, the corps departed for what would turn out to be the worst stretch of trip. By mid-September, winter was setting into the western high country. Food was scarce, and they had to eat several of the packhorses to survive. But once they got over the mountains, they knew the worst was over.

On October 16, they came upon the Columbia River, which took them from the desert to the evergreen forests of the Pacific Northwest. On November 7, 1805, the corps paddled into a huge bay where the Columbia entered into the Pacific Ocean. They had traveled 4,118 miles, according to Clark's figures.

The corps built a shelter, Fort Clatsop, where they spent the winter and prepared for the return trip. In late March, they started home. The group split into two so Clark could explore the Yellowstone River while Lewis looked for a shortcut to the Missouri. Lewis was able to cut about 600 miles and a month's time off their return trip.

The Corps of Discovery reached the Mandan village again in mid-August. Later, when they rode their boats down the St. Louis River, they were greeted by cheering crowds.

In 1805–06, a lieutenant in the U.S. Army named Zebulon Pike explored a large area of the Louisiana Territory. On his second trip Pike followed the Osage and Kansas Rivers west before turning south into Spanish territory.

A Journey to the Southwest

WHILE LEWIS and Clark were looking for the Northwest Passage to the Pacific, a U.S. Army general named James Wilkinson sent a young Army officer on two separate expeditions into the Louisiana Territory.

In the late summer of 1805, Captain Zebulon Pike and 20 soldiers left St. Louis in a 70-foot keelboat. Their mission was to find the **headwaters** of the Mississippi River, an area where French trappers and traders had had free reign for more than a century. Pike was also to select sites for forts, make peace with the Sioux and Ojibwa Indians, and determine the status of British fur traders operating in the newly acquired territory. He would then notify them that the United States government intended to regulate the fur trade from that point forward.

Eleven days after leaving St. Louis, the expedition reached an 11-mile stretch of rapids near what is now Keokuk, Iowa. There they met William Ewing, an American government agent sent to manage Indian affairs. He was traveling with four chiefs and 15 Sauk Indian warriors. Some of the young Sauks helped guide Pike through the rapids. Afterwards, Pike spoke at his first pow-wow. The Sauk seemed pleased with the young man.

On September 4, 1805, the expedition came upon Prairie du Chien. This was the largest settlement in the North Country and one of the most important posts on the frontier. It was situated near where the states of Mississippi and Wisconsin meet. Prairie du Chien had about 600 residents. Most were fur traders and hunters. Pike selected a site nearby for a fort.

Two days away from the outpost, Pike came to the first Sioux village. He met with a Sioux chief named Wabasho, who told Pike his tribe would never fight the Americans because they needed each other.

Soon, Pike could no longer follow the river north. He built a small log fort at Little Falls and left his boats there. Pike and his company of 20 men set off on foot and reached northern Minnesota after six months. He found British fur

This drawing shows an 1825 treaty meeting outside the fort at Prairie du Chien between U.S. government representatives (including William Clark) and leaders of the Chippewa, Sauk, Fox, Menominee, Iowa, Sioux, Winnebago, Ottawa, and Potawatomi tribes. Two decades earlier, Zebulon Pike had established the fort at Prairie du Chien.

traders firmly entrenched in Indian villages there. He informed the natives that the United States now controlled the area and that government agents would be appointed to manage the fur trade.

On February 18, 1806, Pike and his men returned home. Although Pike did not find the headwaters of the Mississippi, he did bring back accurate maps of the country he passed through. His trip also helped strengthen U.S. claims to its vague boundaries in the west.

Pike had barely returned to St. Louis when Wilkinson sent him on another mission, this time to the Southwest. However, this second trip was shrouded with intrigue and betrayal. Unknown to both Pike and President Jefferson, General Wilkinson had become involved in a strange plot to help break western territories away from the United States. He also may have been working as a spy for Spain, which claimed the land to the south of the Louisiana Purchase. Shortly after Pike left, a message was sent to the Spanish governor of Mexico telling him about the explorer.

Pike and his 23 men believed they were on a mission to explore the Arkansas and Red Rivers, to gain information about the Spanish territory that lay at the border, and to display the American flag in the Louisiana Territory.

When the Mexican governor received word of Pike's presence in the territory, he sent 600 cavalrymen to find the Americans. Such a large contingent of soldiers was also designed to impress the natives and demonstrate, quite effectively, who controlled the territory.

In the fall of 1806, Pike and his men pushed through unexplored country filled with hostile Indians. From the Missouri River, Pike traveled overland into Kansas and visited the Osage and Pawnee Indian villages on the way. The Pawnee chief warned Pike that Spanish *dragoons* were looking for his party. Despite the chief's warnings to turn

When Zebulon Pike set out on his two exploratory missions, he had no idea that his boss, General James Wilkinson, was involved in a plot to break western territory away from the United States and create a new country. Eventually, Wilkinson decided the plot would not work. Hoping to save his own reputation, Wilkinson told the president, Thomas Jefferson, about the plot, which had been master-minded by Jefferson's rival, Aaron Burr.

back, however, Pike and his small band continued deeper into the west.

Pike went south to the Arkansas River at the present site of Great Bend, Kansas. On November 9, 1806, Pike counted 96 dead fires at a Spanish campsite and concluded that another large party must have joined the group he followed. He calculated a force of 600. These signs, however, did not deter the explorers. The continued on with their journey.

Six days later, Pike reached the soutnern reaches of the Rocky Mountains, where he spotted the mountain peak that would eventually bear his name. Unfortunately, winter caught the expedition deep among the mountains. The men

Zebulon Pike

Zebulon Montgomery Pike was born January 5, 1779, in Lamberton (now known as Trenton), New Jersey. His father, also named Zebulon, was a captain in the Continental Army, which was fighting the American Revolution against the British.

In 1794, young Zebulon joined the Army, where he was put in charge of barge traffic. He later carried supplies down to the Mississippi River outposts and supervised 12 barges scattered along the Ohio and Mississippi Rivers. In 1799, he was commissioned as a second lieutenant. He also married his cousin, Clarissa.

Early in 1803, Lieutenant Pike became commander of the fort at Kaskaskia in Illinois. He later received orders from General Wilkinson to lead two important missions into the Louisiana Territory.

During the War of 1812, Pike was promoted to the rank of brigadier general. He was killed in 1815 during a successful advance on York, now known as Toronto, Canada.

were not prepared for cold weather, and suffered terrible hardships. Pike and his men did try to climb the mountain, but they were unsuccessful.

Later, Pike's men crossed the Sangre de Cristo Mountains into northern New Mexico. On January 30, 1807, they reached the head-waters of the Rio Grande and followed it south into Spanish territory. In February, Spanish dragoons captured them and escorted Pike to Sante Fe, New Mexico. Though Pike's papers and maps were **confiscated**, he was treated well by the

Like Lewis and Clark, Zebulon Pike found the prairie dogs fascinating. Unfortunately, his men were unable to flush one out of its nest, even though they poured 140 kettles of water into the tunnels.

Spanish. That summer, Pike and his men were released at the border of the Louisiana Territory.

When Pike returned to St. Louis, he was accused of spying for General Wilkinson. He was found to be innocent of any wrongdoing, however. And even though Pike never got his maps back, he was able to remember enough to write a very accurate report about his travels.

The adventures of men like Pike, Lewis and Clark, Mackenzie, Harrod, Boone, and other explorers of the frontier opened the American wilderness for what would follow—a great migration of people west that would soon spread European influence throughout North America.

Chronology

1670 The Hudson Bay Company is created.

1750 Independent traders, mainly French Canadian and Scottish, form the North West Company.

1754 Great Britain and France begin to fight for control of North America. The French and Indian War will last until 1763.

1763 France surrenders Canada to Great Britain, ending the French and Indian War.

1767 Daniel Boone visits Kentucky twice.

1773 Daniel Boone returns to Kentucky and decides to move his family there.

1774 Colonists defeat the Shawnee at the battle of Point Pleasant; Samuel Hearn establishes the first inland Hudson Bay Company outpost; the Transylvania Company sends Daniel Boone to blaze a trail through the Cumberland Gap to Kentucky; Alexander Mackenzie's family moves to North America.

1775 The Revolutionary War begins; Kentucky settlements ask the Continental Congress for recognition.

1778 Siege of Boonesborough; Peter Pond explores the region near Lake Athabasca; Captain James Cook visits Nootka Sound and discovers a freshwater inlet in the vicinity of present-day Anchorage, Alaska.

Chronology

1779 20,000 new settlers move to Kentucky; Mackenzie begins working with Finlay, Gregory & MacLeod; Pond becomes a partner in the North West Company.

1785 XY Company merges with the North West Company; Mackenzie becomes a minor partner in the new firm.

1791 Mackenzie enrolls in Cambridge University to study navigation and astronomy in preparation for another journey westward.

1793 Mackenzie and his entourage reach the Pacific July 22.

1803 The United States buys the Louisiana Territory from France; President Thomas Jefferson sends Meriwether Lewis and William Clark in search of a northwest passage to the Pacific Ocean.

1804 In April, Lewis and Clark, with the Corps of Discovery, start their journey up the Missouri River.

1805 The Lewis and Clark expedition reaches the Pacific Ocean; General James Wilkinson sends Zebulon Pike to find the headwaters of the Mississippi River.

1806 The Corps of Discovery returns to St. Louis in September; General Wilkinson sends Pike to explore the headwaters of the Arkansas and Red Rivers.

1816 Daniel Boone continues exploring the West, possibly reaching Idaho.

Glossary

Breeches—short pants covering the hips and thighs and fitting snugly just below the knee.

Brine—water that is heavily loaded with salt.

Chronometer—a device designed to keep highly accurate time.

Circumnavigate—to go completely around.

Commerce—a large-scale exchange or buying and selling of goods.

Confiscate—to take somebody's property legally.

Dragoon—a member of a European military unit made up of heavily armed mounted troops.

Encroach—to intrude gradually, taking away somebody's authority, rights, or property.

Garrison—a military post.

Gauntlet—a form or punishment in which the person to be punished is forced to run between two lines of men, who beat him as he passed.

Headwaters—the source of a stream or river.

Keelboat—a shallow, covered boat used for freight that is rowed, poled, or towed.

Glossary

Longitude—the angular distance east or west of the prime meridian that stretches from the North Pole to the South Pole. Determining longitude helps explorers understand where they are.

Pelt—the skin of an animal.

Pirogues—a boat made by hollowing out a large log.

Preservative—an additive used to protect against decay.

Rival—one who strives for a competitive advantage or to have what another wants.

Sextant—an instrument for measuring angular distances, used especially in navigation to observe the positions of stars.

Siege—a military blockade of an area designed to force surrender.

Smallpox—a highly contagious disease caused by a virus.

Stipulation—a condition, requirement, or item specified in an agreement.

Stockade—a tall enclosure made of wooden posts driven into the ground side by side.

Further Reading

Coues, Elliott. *The Expeditions of Zebulon Montgomery Pike*. New York: Dover Publications, 1987.

Edwards, Judith. *Lewis and Clark's Journey of Discovery in American History*. Springfield, N.J.: Enslow Publishers Inc., 1999.

Hall, Eleanor J. *The Lewis and Clark Expedition*. San Diego: Lucent Books, 1996.

Hammon, Neal O., editor. *My Father, Daniel Boone: The Draper Interviews*. Lexington: The University Press of Kentucky, 1999.

Kozar, Richard. *Daniel Boone and the Exploration of the Frontier*. Philadelphia: Chelsea House Publishers, 2000.

Mackenzie, Alexander. *Journal of the Voyage to the Pacific*. Edited by Walter Sheppe. New York: Dover Publications, 1995.

Internet Resources

Daniel Boone
http://www.berksweb.com/boonetext.html
http://memory.loc.gov/ammem/today/jun07.html

Alexander Mackenzie
http://www.calverley.dawson-creek.bc.ca
http://www.cbe.ab.ca/b379/projects/explorers/mackenzie.htm

Lewis and Clark
http://www.nps.gov/lecl/
http://www.pbs.org/lewisandclark/

Zebulon Pike
http://www.kcmuseum.com/explor05.html
http://dlwgraphics.com/mnpike2.htm

Index

Photo Credits

About the Author

DIANE COOK is an award-winning journalist and the former publisher of a monthly Christian newspaper. Her articles have appeared in the *Delaware State Chamber of Commerce Business Journal, Delaware Today, Corrections Technology, Family Digest,* and the *Army, Air Force, Navy and Marine Corps Times.* Her stories have been posted online at Discovery Travel News, Globest.com, Tradeweave, AOL Digital City, and Internetcontent.net. In her free time, she writes sketches, plays, and puppet shows. She lives near Dover, Delaware, with her husband, David, and their three children, Leslie, Matthew, and Nathan.